CHAMBERS
OF
DELIGHT

LUCINDA LAMBTON

GORDON FRASER

First published in 1983 by
The Gordon Fraser Gallery Ltd, London and Bedford
Photographs copyright © Lucinda Lambton 1983

BRITISH LIBRARY CATALOGUING IN PUBLICATION DATA
Lambton, Lucinda
  Chambers of Delight
  1. Chamber pots—History—Pictorial works
  I. Title
  749'.3   NK695.C5

ISBN 0–86092–063–1

FRONT COVER

left:
Numbers 73 and 42

right:
French mahogany pot cupboard with gilt bronze
wreath, *c.* 1810, at Belvoir Castle in Leicestershire.
  The vast early eighteenth-century bed, its
contemporary hangings and the Chinese silk on the
walls all came from the old Belvoir before it was
rebuilt (between 1800 and 1830) by James Wyatt
and Sir John Thoroton, with interiors by Benjamin
Dean Wyatt and Matthew Cotes Wyatt.

BACK COVER
From the collection at Newby Hall

Set in 'Monophoto' Apollo 645 and 665 by Keyspools Ltd, Golborne Lancs
and printed at Toppan Printing Co. Ltd, Japan
Designed by Chrissie Charlton

CHAMBER POTS IN LITERATURE:

AN ANTHOLOGY

The horsemen of the Sybarites, more than 5000 strong, paraded with saffron-coloured coats over their breast-plates, and in the summer their young men journeyed to the grottoes of the nymphes on the Lusias river and there spent the time in every form of luxury. Whenever the wealthy among them went for a vacation to the country they took three days to finish the one-day journey, although they travelled in carriages. Further, some of their roads leading to the country were roofed over. Most of them own wine cellars near the sea shore, into which the wines are sent through pipes from their country-estates; part of it is sold outside the country, part of it, again is carried over the city in boats. They also hold many public banquets at frequent intervals, and they reward with golden crowns the men who have striven brilliantly for honours, and publish their values at the State sacrifices and games, proclaiming not so much their loyalty to the State as their service in providing dinners; on these occasions they crown even the cooks who have most skilfully concocted the dishes served. Among the Sybarites were also devised tubs in which they lay and enjoyed vapour baths. They, too, were the first to invent chamber pots, which they carried to their drinking parties ... To such a point had they carried their luxurious refinement that they even trained their horses to dance at their feasts to the accompaniment of pipes.

Athenaeus: Deipnosophists, XII

It is a token of speciall kindness, to this day among the best men in France, to reduce a Syllogisme *in Bocardo* together. Insomuch as I have heard it seriously tolde, that a great Magnifico of Venice, being Ambassador in France, and hearing a Noble person was come to speake with him, made him stay til he had untyed his points: and when he was new set on his stoole, sent for the Noble man to come to him at that time; as a verie speciall favour.

For I happening to demand of a deare friend of mine, concerning a great companion of his, whether he were religious or no, and namely if he used to pray: he tolde me that to his remembrance he never heard him aske any thing of God, nor thanke God for any thing: except it were once at a Jakes, he heard him say, he thanked God he had had a good stoole. This you see, a good stoole might move as great devotion in some man, as a bad sermon; & sure it sutes very well, that *Quorn Deas est venter, eorum templum, sit cloaca.* He that makes his belly his god, I would have him make a Jakes his chappell. But he that would indeed call to minde, how *Arrius*, that notable and famous, or rather infamous hereticke, came to his miserable end upon a Jakes: might take just occasion even at that homely

businesse, to have godly thoughts: rather than some have, wanton, or most have, idle. To which purpose I remember in my riming dayes, I wrote a short Elegie upon a homely Embleme: which both verse and Embleme, they have set up in *Cloacinas* chappell, at my house very solemnely.

of Sir Thomas More's humour ... he had spirite ... When the king sent to him to know if he had changed his mind, he announced yea: the king sent straight a councellor to him, to take his subscription to the six Articles. Oh said he I have not changed my minde in that matter, but only in this: I thought to have sent for a Barber, to have been shaven ere I had died, but now if it please the king, he shall cut off head, and beard, and all together ... after this one coming to him of good will, to tell him he must prepare him to dye, for he could not live: he called for his urinale and having made water in it he cast it and viewed it (as Physicians do) a pretty while; at last he swore soberly that he saw nothing in that mans water but that he might live, if it pleased the king.

Sir John Harington's A New Discourse of a Stale Subject, Called The Metamorphosis of Ajax (1596) Edited by Elizabeth Story Donno, Routledge & Kegan Paul, London, 1962, pp. 91–3

He that writes the first book of Samuel tels that David did cut off the lap of Saules coate, and leaves not to tell, what Saul was then doing. The writer of Bassianus life telles, how he was not onely privily murdred, but murdred at the privy. Heliogabulus body was throwne into a Jakes, as writeth Suetonius. Lastly the best, and the best written part of all our Chronicles, in all mens opinions; is that of Richard the third, written as I have heard by Moorton, but as most suppose, by that worthy, and uncorrupt Magistrate Sir Thomas More, sometime Lord Chancelor of England, where it is written; how the king was devising with Teril, how to have his nephewes privily murdred, & it is added, he was sitting on a draught (a fit carpet for such a counsil.)

Ibid, pp. 107–8

... there are three things that make a man wary of his house, a smoking chimney, a dropping eves, and a brauling woman. I would no less willingly avoid them, but when the stormes come, I must as my neighbours do, beare that with patience, which I can not reforme with choler, and learne of the good

Socrates, who when Xantippe had crowned him with a chamber-pot, he bare it off single with his head and shoulders, and said to such as laughed at him for it:

It never yet was deemed a wonder
  To see that raine should follow thunder.

Ibid, pp. 152–3

Oh split my hart, least it doe breake with rage
To see th'immodest looseness of our age . . . .
When *Hermus* makes a worthy question,
Whether of *Wright*, as *Paraphonalion*
A silver pispot fits his Lady dame?
Or is't too good? a pewter best became.

The Scourge of Villanie, Satyre II: 'Difficile
est Satyram non scribere', lines 69–140.
John Marston (1599), John Lane, Bodley
Head, London, 1925

Harrigo, a siker English Gentleman attending the English Embassador – Serulina a beauteous virgin. In Spain 1663

SERUL 'tis sweet being in the Country with all this; and when I marry it shall be to become a Wife, not a Slave, Don *Harrigo*.

HAR. That's resolv'd as I could wish; and for the Country, 'tis no question but 'tis sweet as Lavander or Rose-Mary can make it; but I think the Orange and Jassimine in a bottle, and the Trees all the year in your house at *Madrid*, as sweet as those in the hedges.

SERUL I, but to walk and gather these flowers, is there no pleasure in that?

HAR. When? by Moon-Shine? I am quite sure you dare not meet Signior *Sol* abroad, unless you'l come home, like Rose-cakes from a Still, bak'd and sweating; which though your dew can be sweet (as common civility will make us allow that) yet 'tis troublesome and a new sight to meet Ladies abroad, when the dogs cry as they pass the streets, when to walk in your Court but two turns is evidence for chastity, and out-doors the old Law *Ordeal*: 'Tis enough to endure such stabs as the Sun strikes in the Dog-days: 'tis true, they say he will beat the hoof in his woollen-hose, till his feet sweat and stink more then a hunted Bores, and are fain to be steep'd at night as long as the Beef, ere they be fresh again: this commonly out of freedom is done in my Wifes Chamber: and if he be kind, and dares trust you, perhaps he desires you to cut his Corns and dress his Issue, signs of favour I can assure you; and such as you must not hope, unless your woman be out of the way; and that honor being pass'd the Gyant stretches himself, yawns and sighs a belch or two, stales in your pot, farts as loud as a Musket for a jest: and then throws himself under the Rug, and expects you in his foul sheets, and aspitting

cloath, where hangs as much of his Lungs as remains in his body; and ere you can get into the bed he calls you with a snore or two; and are not these fine things in a Ladies bed? Who would not rejoice to meet his woollen-waste-coat and knit-night-cap without a lining? a shirt so nasty a cleanly ghost would scarce appear in at the latter day; for his linin is a kin to him ere he puts it off; thus prepar'd for delight you Ladies meet your Country husbands, the *Alphonso*, high shooes; and there lye and suffer them to abuse you as often as they please to use you which you'l too late repent; and there you may lye and sigh whole nights away, he'l snore and snore till it be day under the same covers, and in the same bed his forefathers liv'd and dy'd in, and some so lately you may smell the very earthiness of the Corps still; and 'tis a better favour than his arms or breath, a stink composed of vile Tobacco and dead Wine, stuffed nose, rotten lungs, and hollow teeth, half whos number has been drawn with dry Cheese, and tuff lean beef; yet this man you must kiss; nay you must kiss none but this, and muzzle through his beard to find his lips; and this you can submit to for threescore year for a joynture; which you must purchase too; for he sells you that and this Paradise his bed, for the price of your portion only, and in strict sence you give him so much to lye with him as long as he lives; for unless he dies you have nothing but a place in his Family, and so has his dog, who shall have a pension as well as you.

Tomaso or *The Wanderer*, The Second Part,
A Comedy, Thomas Killigrew, London,
1663.

Of the luxury and expense of some Persons in Apparel, and their variety and vanity therin, and in their other furniture.

Heliogbalus the Emperour excelled all others in his prodigious Luxury . . . for his upper Garments were ever either of Gold or Purple, or else the richest Silks that were procurable, nay sometimes all beset with Jewels and Pearls, which habit he was the first that brought up in Rome; his Shoos were bedecked with Precious Stones and Pearle: he never wore any suit of Apparel twice. He thought of wearing a Diadem made up with Jewels, wherewith to set off his face, and render his aspect more effeminate. He sate commonly amongst Flowers or the most precious odours: – his excrements he discharged into Gold vessels, and Urined in Vessels of Onyx, or Myrrhine pots. He never swimmed but in Fishpools, that were beforehand replete with the Nobler Ungents, and tinged with Saffron. His Household-stuff was Gold or Silver, his Bedsteads, Tables and Chests of Massy Silver, and so were his Cauldrons and other Pots; and even these and the most part of his other vessels, had lascivious engravings represented on the sides of them.

The Wonders of the Little World, Rev.
Nathaniel Wanley, London, 1678

4

High officials of Corea urinate in public into brass bowls, which are carried by attendants in sort of net or fillet and presented when required.

Scatalogic Rites of All Nations, John G. Bourke, Washington D.C., 1891

From The Lady's Dressing Room 1730

Why *Strephon* will you tell the rest?
And must you needs describe the Chest?
That careless Wench! no Creature warn her
To move it out from yonder corner;
But leave it standing in full Sight,
For you to exercise your Spight.
In vain the Workman shew'd his Wit
With Rings and Hinges counterfeit
To make it seem in this Disguise,
A Cabinet to vulgar Eyes;
Which *Strephon* ventur'd to look in,
Resolv'd to go thro' thick and thin;
He lifts the Lid; there needs no more,
He smelt it all the Time before.
As, from within Pandora's Box,
When *Epimetheus* op'd the Locks,
A sudden universal Crew
Of humane Evils upward flew;
He still was comforted to find
That *Hope* at last remain'd behind;
So *Strephon* lifting up the Lid,
To view what in the Chest was hid,
The Vapours flew from out the Vent,
But *Strephon* cautious never meant
The Bottom of the Pan to grope,
And fowl his Hands in Search of *Hope*.
O ne'er may such a vile Machine
Be once in *Celia's* Chamber seen!
O may she better learn to keep
'Those Secrets of the hoary deep!'

As Mutton-Cutlets, Prime of Meat,
Which tho' with Art you salt and beat,
As Laws of Cookery require,
And roast them at the clearest Fire;
If from adown the hopeful Chops
The Fat upon the Cinder drops,
To stinking smoak it turns to Flame
Pois'ning the Flesh from whence it came;
And up exhales a greasy Stench,
For which you curse the careless Wench;
So Things which must not be exprest,
When plumpt into the reeking Chest;
Send up an excremental Smell
To taint the Parts from whence they fell.
The Pettycoats and Gown perfume,
And waft a Stink round every Room.

Thus finishing his grand Survey,
The Swain, disgusted, slunk away,
Repeating in his am'rous fits,
'Oh! Celia, Celia, Celia sh — —!'

Poetical Works, Jonathan Swift, ed. Herbert Davis, Oxford University Press, 1967

And now, dear Mary, we have got to Haddingborrough, among the Scots, who are civil enuff for our money ... — But they should not go for to impose upon foreigners; for the bills in their houses say they have different *easements* to let; and behold there is nurro geaks in the whole kingdom, nor anything for pore sarvants, but a barrel with a pair of tongs thrown a-cross; and all the chairs in the family are emptied into this here barrel once a-day; and at ten o'clock at night the whole cargo is flung out of a back windore that looks into some street or lane, and the maid calls *Gardy Loo* to the passengers, which signifies *Lord have mercy upon you*! and this is done every night in every house in Haddingborrough; as you may guess, Mary Jones, what a sweet savour comes from such a number of profuming pans; but they say it is wholesome, and, truly, I believe it is; for being in the vapours, and thinking of Issabel and Mr Clinker, I was going into a fit of astericks, when this piss, saving your presence, took me by the nose so powerfully, that I sneezed three times, and found myself wonderfully refreshed; and this to be sure is the raisin why there are no fits in Haddingborrough.

Humphrey Clinker, Tobias Smollet (1771) Oxford University Press, 1966

... till the year 1760 there was no such thing as a privy in Madrid, the metropolis of Spain ... Before that time it was universal practice to throw the ordure out of the windows, during the night, into the street, where numbers of men were employed to remove it ... His present Catholic Majesty, having determined to free his capital from so gross a nuisance, ordered by proclamation, that the proprietor of every house should build a privy, and that sinks, drains, and common-sewers should be made at the public expense. The Spaniards, though long accustomed to an arbitrary government, resented this proclamation with great spirit, as an infringement of the common rights of mankind, and made a vigorous struggle against it being carried into execution. Every class devised some objection against it, but the physicians bid the fairest to interest the King in the preservation of the ancient priviledges of his people; for they remonstrated that if the filth was not, as usual, thrown into the streets, a fatal sickness would probably ensue, because of the putrescent particles of the air, which such filth attracted, would then be imbibed by the human body. But this expedient, with every other that could be thought of, proved unsuccessful, and the popular discontent then ran so high that it was very near producing an insurrection; his majesty, however, at length prevailed, and Madrid is now as clear as most of the considerable cities in Europe. But many of the citizens, probably upon the principles advanced by their physicians, that heaps of filth prevent deleterious particles of air from fixing upon neighbouring substances, have, to keep their food wholesome, constructed their privies by the kitchen fire.

An Account of the Voyages undertaken by the order of this Present Majesty for making Discoveries in the Southern Hemisphere, John Hawkesworth, 3 vols, London, 1773

Of the Pot-cupboard

These are used in genteel bed-rooms, and are sometimes finished in Satin-wood, and in a style a little elevated above their use, the two drawers below the cupboard are real. The partitions may be cross-banded, and a string round the corners of the drawer. These feet are turned, but sometimes they are made square. Sometimes there are folding doors to the cupboard part, and sometimes a curtain of a green silk, fixed on a brass wire at top and bottom, but in this design a tambour door is used as preferable. The upper cupboard contains shelves, and is intended to keep medicines to be taken in the night, or to hold other little articles which servants are not permitted to overlook.

The Cabinet Maker and Upholsterer's Drawing Book, Thomas Sheraton, London, 1793

Chamber Pot: . . . The Sybarites invented them because they would not be at the trouble of moving. They were chiefly of glass, but sometimes of metal or pottery, and were of the form of boats for women. The Romans had them brought by snapping their fingers. One for Queen Elizabeth was of silver. The form was sometimes a truncated cone with a large handle.

Urine: Vases called *bastra*, for relief of passengers, were placed by the Romans upon the edges of roads and streets.

Encyclopedia of Antiquities, Rev. Thomas Dudley Fosbroke MA FSA, London, 1825

GREAT COMFORT TO INVALIDS. 'FYFE's patent hermetically sealed commode pail, forming with its mahogany seat and earthen pan, a completely air-tight, moderous, portable chamber closet, for £1. 13s.; in a neat japanned box £2. 9s.; in a handsome mahogany enclosure: £3; rendering a sick room at all times, as fresh and comfortable to enter as a well-appointed drawing room.' Sold at FYFE's repository, 26 Tavistock Street, Covent Garden.

The Builder, 31 December 1842

In country places people open their doors and windows abundantly and the house is made fresh. This cannot be safely done in London, and houses, if not very large, smell musty, while the bedrooms smell of human exudations. This is especially so in inns: no inn which the writer has found in London except in two or three instances where the house or the furniture was perfectly new, gave a bed-room perfectly fresh. Coming to the great capital, as a rule you cannot get a bed to rest without nausea, and endurance takes the place of comfort.

Record of the International Exhibition, Dr R. Angus Smith FRS, 1862

'Come take away, and lets to bedde, yee shall have cleane sheets Ned: but they be coarse, good strong hempe, of my daughters own spinning. And I tell thee, your chamber pot, must be a fair horn, a badge of our occupation; for we buy no bending Peauter, nor bending earth.'

Haywood, *I King Edward the Fourth*, 1600 from *Scatalogic Rites of All Nations*, John G. Bourke, Washington D.C., 1891, p. 139

Enter	Toby *Coachman, with a Urinal*
NON.	How now! What have you there, Sirrah?
TOB.	An't please your Worship 'tis my Water; I had a Spice o'th new Disease i'th House, and so carried it to Master Doctor.
NON.	Well; and what did he say to you?
TOB.	He told me very sad News, and please you: I am somewhat bashful to speak on't.
ISA.	Out with it Man.
TOB.	Why truly he told me, the Party that own'd the Water, was with Child.

The Wild Gallant, J. Dryden, 1663

I found no body in my Lords Chamber. There was a Closet there, in which was a Close Stool, and that I found shut, and thinking my Lord was there, I would not disturb my Lord, but came down again and stayed a little while, in so much as I thought my Lord by that time might have been come out. I went up again and found no body in the Chamber, but the Closet Door shut still, I went against the Door and knocked three times and said, My Lord, My Lord, and no body answered; Then I looked through the chink of the door, between the Door and the Wall, and I could see blood, and a little part of the Razour. Then I called to the Warder and the People of the House, and they came up and found him there.

Tryal of Laurence Bradden and Hugh Speke, 1684

'Our Ladies in England are asham'd of being seen even in going to or returning from the most necessary parts of our houses, as it was in itself shameful to do even in private, what nature absolutely requires at certain seasons to be done: whereas I have known an old woman in Holland set herself on the next hole to a Gentleman, and civilly offer him her mussel shell by way of scraper after she had done with it herself. Thus you know it is no indecency for a man in the streets and even before women, to turn his face against the wall and do what it would be reckon'd very immodest in any lady to do, how loaded and uneasy soever she might be.

That men very early had places of retirement built or set apart for the easing of nature in, and that they had likewise vessels of the same kind or however for the same purposes, as our closestool pans, and chamber-pots and bed-pans, may be made out beyond dispute. Nature from the beginning of the world taught men the decency of retiring in order to ease themselves, and conveniency very soon taught them the use of particular apartments to retire to.'

A Philosophical Dialogue concerning Decency, S. Rolleston, 1751

It would be a desirable object, in houses which are not provided with water-closets, that every individual were furnished with his own night-chair, as most of the common places of retirement are literally ventilators, where some parts of the body are exposed to a current of air, which is frequently the cause of disorders, particularly in persons subject to colds, and all other complaints originating from supressed perspiration ... Men who are troubled with the piles ... ought to be very careful in resorting to such places. – In the usual privies, there generally prevails in summer a pestilential fetor, so that it becomes almost impossible to wait for the proper evacuation, both because of the disagreeable smell, and the danger of being infected with disease.

Lectures on Diet and Regimen, A. F. M. Willich, 1779

As soon as the different members of the family are assembled at breakfast, the housemaid should repair to the bed-chambers, open the windows (unless the weather be damp), draw the curtains up to the head of the bed, throw the bed clothes upon two chairs placed at the foot of each bed, and leave the feather beds open to the air. When this has been done in all the rooms in use, she should then bring her chamber-bucket, with a jug of hot water, and with the proper towels, empty and clean out all the chamber vessels in each room, and then instantly carry off, empty and wash out the bucket, and turn it down in some appropriate place, that the water may completely run off from it.

A New System of Practical Domestic Economy, H. Colburn, 1823. This and the previous four extracts are all in Selina's Aunt, J. Hetherington, Birmingham, 1965

Almost as important as the bed itself was the chamber-pot beneath it, perhaps the most necessary of all utensils in an age which had as yet no proper drainage or sanitation. Hogarth himself was not particularly scrupulous in his personal habits; on one occasion he pulled down his breeches and squatted down over a grave, at which his companion slashed at his bare rump with a bunch of stinging nettles and 'Hogarth finished his business against the church door'. In his picture of London by night he showed the unpopular Thomas de Veil receiving the contents of a chamber-pot on his head, traditionally one of the hazards of town life. . . .

England in the Age of Hogarth, Derek Jarrett, London, 1974

ACKNOWLEDGMENTS

I would like to thank the following people for their unfailing kindness during the preparation of this book:

John Coleman
Mr and Mrs Robin Compton
Paul Duffie
Patrick and Anthea Forde
Tony Herbert
Amanda Herries
Myles Hildyard
The Duke and Duchess of Marlborough
Sarah Medlam
The Duke and Duchess of Northumberland

Mr and Mrs Joe Painter
Mrs Doreen Ramshaw
Patricia Rawlings
Victoria de Rin
David Robottam
The Duke of Rutland
Roland Smith
Elizabeth Steele
Rory Ward-Roper

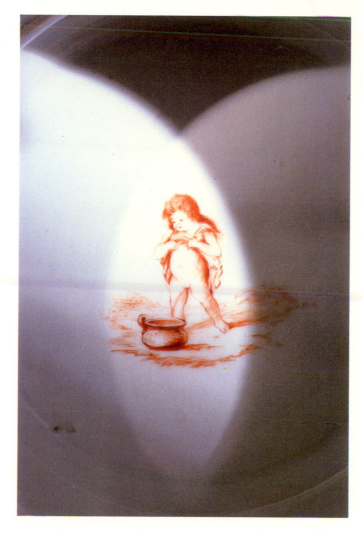

1 Angoulême porcelain chamber pot,
c. 1780, by Dihl and Guerhard, rue de Boudy, Paris.
   From collection made by Robert de Vyner
(1842–1915).
Newby Hall, Yorkshire

2 Transfer printed, 1850s Yorkshire. There are four pictures under the inside rim: 'Going to the Races' with a flower-bedecked cart, a fiddle, a dog and a bottle; 'Love and Beauty' with a small white man embracing an immense black woman; The Repentance' with a man clutching his wife, both of them in nightcaps and shirts; and 'Married Life' with a weedy-looking man being kicked and beaten by his wife with a poker. On the side are the verses 'To the Wife' and 'A Present'.

3 Nineteenth-century Staffordshire Napoleonic cartoon pot. There is no external decoration. *Newby Hall, Yorkshire*

4 'A Present for James'. Transfer-printed
Staffordshire pots of the 1830s.
Newby Hall, Yorkshire

5 'Morning and Evening Exercises'. A pot of the
1830s.
Patricia Rawlings Private Collection

11

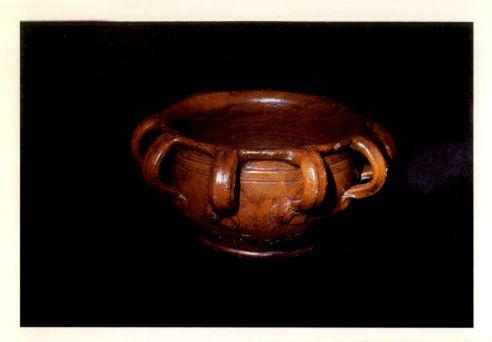

6 Yorkshire peasant ware. Nineteenth-century
nine-handled, lead-glazed earthenware, with 'Hand
it over to me my dear' incised around the base.
Inside, there is a band of unglazed pottery.
Newby Hall, Yorkshire

7 Part of the collection of the seventeenth-century
earthenware pots in the Museum of London, dating
from as early as 1600; the earliest is on the bottom
right in 'Tudor Greenglaze'. This same shape
continued throughout the seventeenth century.
The taller tend to be earlier, the smaller and flatter,
later.

8 Pewter pots from the middle to second half of the seventeenth century, with pewterers' marks.
Museum of London

9 Three 'Metropolitan' slipware ornamental pieces dating from 1630 to 1680 with pipe clay decoration, which turns yellow under the lead glaze. They were made largely around the Harlow area and given the name Metropolitan because they were sent to London.
Museum of London

13

10 Blue, gold and Terracotta Imari Chinese pots of the eighteenth century.
Newby Hall, Yorkshire

11 Quarter-size brown and white Staffordshire of the 1840s.
Patricia Rawlings Private Collection

13 'The Emperor'. Regimental nickname for the silver chamber pot belonging to Joseph Bonaparte, King of Spain, and captured by the 14th (King's) Hussars at the battle of Vittoria, 21 June 1813. It is still in the hands of the 14th/20th (King's) Hussars, who are consequently known as 'The Emperor's Chambermaids'.

12 1770s sideboard, by Robert Adam, at Saltram in Devon. This piece of furniture is unusual in that it is built into the room. Beneath the urn which was used as a wine cooler there are shelves for chamber pots for gentlemen's after-dinner relief. Saltram, built in the mid-eighteenth century, is a remarkable survival of that period, having remained unaltered during the nineteenth century.

14 and 15 Nineteenth-century step commode, one of many at Belvoir Castle in Leicestershire. This is one of the King's rooms, a suite always used by visiting members of the Royal Family. The Prince Regent, Edward VII and the Duke of Windsor have all slept here.

The bed and Chinese wallpaper are contemporary with the rebuilding of Belvoir between 1800 and 1830 when the Fifth Duke of Rutland employed James Wyatt, Sir John Thoroton, Benjeman Dean and Matthew Cotes Wyatt to design this romantic castle.

16 William IV mahogany and ebonised pot cupboard in the form of a tuncated column, 1830–37. In the library as the dining room was being repainted, it would normally have stood by the sideboard to be made use of by the gentlemen when the ladies had retired after dinner.

The portrait is of Lady Mary Sackville by Lely, c. 1680. The curtains are of glazed wool damask made in Norwich in the nineteenth century. The mahogany dumb waiter is George III. The pine panelled walls of 1780 are by John Carr of York. *Raby Castle, County Durham*

17 Staffordshire piece, *c*. 1805. Possibly associated with the Napoleonic Wars. On one side the verse:

> Here's to you Jack
> With all my heart
> We'el have a glass
> Before we part
> Success to the tars of Old England.
> On the other:
> My heart is fixed
> I cannot range
> I love my choice
> Too well to change

As well as

> Columbus the largest ship ever built
> Berthing 6000 Tons
> Length   301 Feet
> Breadth   50 Feet
> Depth   29 Feet

Old Oak Inn, Hutton Magna, Yorkshire

18 Leeds creamware, orange and brown design on cream, 1827.
Newby Hall, Yorkshire

19, 20 and 21 Sunderland Ware Lustre Pot. Made at the Garrison Factory, 1850.
Patricia Rawlings Private Collection

22, 23 and 24 Three views of a transfer-printed
Staffordshire of 1850–60. A magnificently large pot,
it measures some 18 inches across. It is unusual to
find such an elaborate design on the outside base.
Patricia Rawlings Private Collection

25 Another giant, some two feet across. Staffordshire of the 1830s, with two miniature mocha ware pots. The process of mocha ware is when the surface tension of the slip is broken by acid and alkaline reaction. Originally discovered when tobacco was spat onto the alkaline slip; tobacco heated with boiling water becomes nicotinic acid, which (combined with a metallic oxide for colour) spreads out when applied to the pot, producing its own strange patterns.
Newby Hall, Yorkshire

26 'Anti splash thunder bowl' Staffordshire 1830s
potted by Arthur Wood.
Joe Painter, Dersingham, Norfolk

27 and 28 Crimean War commemorative
Sunderland lustre frog pot.
Newby Hall, Yorkshire

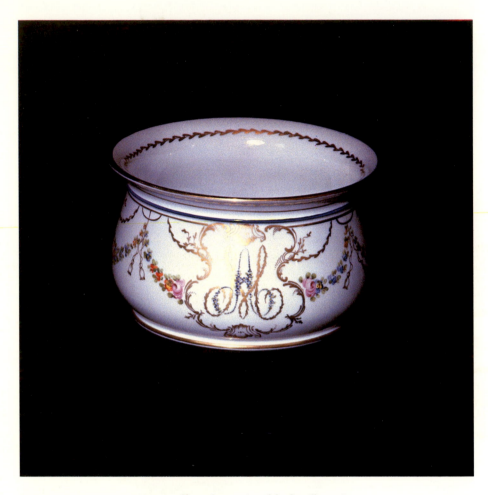

29 Angoulême: the exterior of the first illustration
in the book (p. 9). Porcelain of *c*. 1780 with Marie
Antoinette.
  By Dihl and Sunderland, rue de Bouby, Paris.
Newby Hall, Yorkshire

30 and 31 The nineteenth-century bedside steps at Alnwick castle in Northumberland. The pot was kept in a compartment behind the top step; the middle step pulled out to reveal a commode when the lid was lifted. The
gilt canopied bed is late eighteenth
century. The pictures are of Maria,
Countess of Coventry, Mr Duters, Tutor
to Lord Algernon Percy, 'An Old Lady' and two
portraits of the second Duke of Northumberland.

The pot, c. 1800, is porcelain.

32 Nineteenth-century bed bottle for gentlemen, at Seaforde in Co. Down, N. Ireland.

33 1850s Coalport-style bedpan. *Alnwick Castle, Northumberland.*

34 A pot cupboard behind the shutters in the dining room at Flintham Hall in Nottinghamshire. When the house was lavishly Victorianised between 1853 and 1857 by T. C. Hine, the cupboards were built into the oak panelling for the relief of gentlemen after dinner.

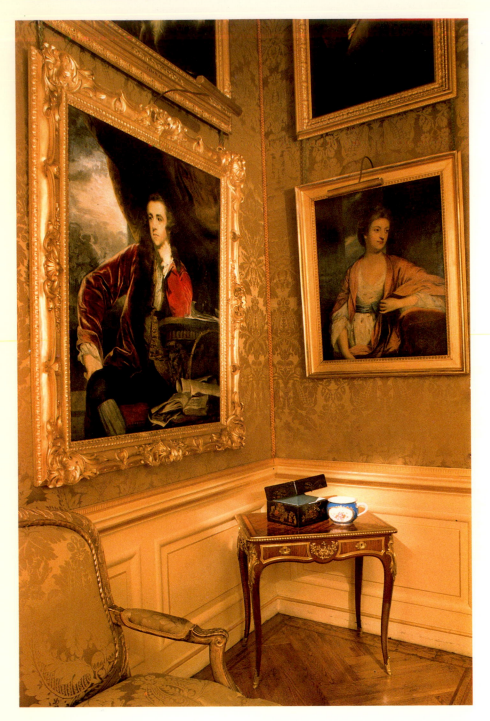

35 Marie Antoinette's gilt-enriched Sèvres porcelain travelling pot of 1758, decorated by Binet. Small and neat, only six inches in diameter, it has a black and gold case decorated in the Chinese taste.

The table is Louis XV mahogany and kingwood with an inlaid marquetry top and ormolu mouldings.

The portraits are of Elizabeth, Countess of Pembroke (1757–1831) and Francis, Marquis of Tavistock by Sir Joshua Reynolds.

The chair is part of a Louis XV salon suite.
Green drawing room, Blenheim Palace, Oxfordshire

36 and 37 A painted wood box close stool of 1825.
With brass-handled and hinged mahogany seat
board.
W. Stockbridge and Sons Ltd, Cambridge

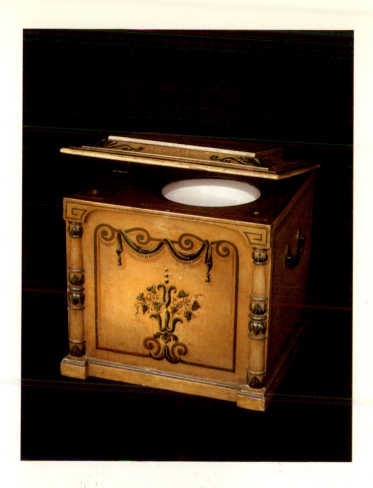

38 and 39 Sunderland ware frog pot. Originally made to amuse with the liquid creating a glugging sound as it passed the frog in a mug. In a pot these effects are less appealing.

This is a marriage pot given as a joke to newly-weds. It is of orange rather than mauve and pink lustre and made by Ball Brothers in the 1850s. On the other side is the verse 'Present'.
Patricia Rawlings Private Collection

40 Rouge de Feu Japanese Imari pottery of the
nineteenth century. The pot at the top is
considerably earlier. The Japanese copied all the
best Chinese work, making very good pieces in the
nineteenth century.
Newby Hall, Yorkshire

41 and 42 Nineteenth-century barge ware, inside
and out. These pots made for bargees were always
lavishly, if sometimes inconveniently, applied with
encrusted decoration.
Newby Hall, Yorkshire

43 Sunderland ware. Garrison pottery of 1850. On the side of this pot with a miserable picture of a weeping woman with two children waving to a ship, 'The Sailors Farewell': 'Sweet oh sweet is that sensation, when two hearts in union meet, but the pains of separation, tingles bitter with the sweet.' On the other side is a mariner's compass.
Newby Hall, Yorkshire

44 and 45 A Sunderland frog mug intended to make vile noises when emptied. Made at the Garrison Pottery in the 1850s. Of the same date is the Sunderland ware lustre pot in glimmering mauve and pink, also from the Garrison Pottery. On the other side is another 'Present' verse and inside a figure in a pyjama jacket with the words: 'Use me well, keep me clean, I will not tell what I have seen'.
Patricia Rawlings Private Collection

46 A selection of mid-nineteenth-century Masons Ironstone, with the distinctive snake handles. The little pot below is Staffordshire, 1830. The insides are all blank except for the rims.
Patricia Rawlings Private Collection

47 Two miniature transfer-printed Staffordshire pieces of the 1830s. 'For a kiss I'll hand you this'
and
'Pass it this way my dear'
Patricia Rawlings Private Collection

48 and 49 Turn of the century bronze cigar-cutter (open and closed), bought in Edinburgh in 1975.
Patricia Rawlings Private Collection

50 Possibly Sewell. Brilliantly coloured miniature of the eighteenth century.
Patricia Rawlings Private Collection

51 Nineteenth-century pillar commode. A pretty
piece of furniture when closed, with a beadwork
top to the lid and only the knob of the step to give a
clue to its identity.
Private Collection

52 Nineteenth-century shell design.
Oak Tree Inn, Hutton Magna, Yorkshire

53 Marble ware, mid-nineteenth century, potted
by G. L. Ashworth and Brothers Ltd, Hanley.
Joe Painter, Dersingham, Norfolk

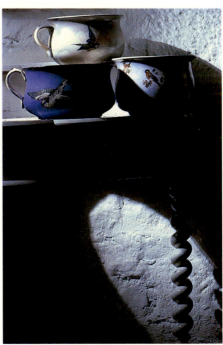

54 A collection of Rileys, Rogers and Spode chamber pots, all dating from about 1830 except for the Wedgewood (middle, second from bottom), which, stamped 'Etruria England', dates from the 1870s.
Patricia Rawlings Private Collection

55 Three pots from Scots pottery Methuen which flourished between 1837 and 1864.
Oak Tree Inn, Hutton Magna, Yorkshire

56 Pretending plate bucket – elegantly concealing a dining-room pot from the early nineteenth century, at Seaforde near Co. Down, N. Ireland.

The pictures are three generations of eighteenth-century Matthew Fordes. The sideboard and the French centrepiece are both Regency.

Seaforde was built in 1816.

57 and 58 The inside and bottom of a nineteenth-
century Kate Greenaway pot.
Anglesey Toy Museum

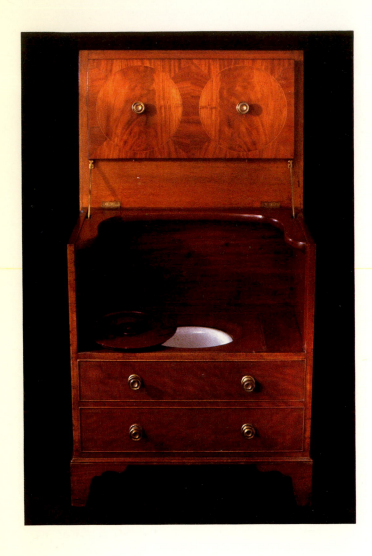

59 and 60 Mahogany commode, veneered with
mahogany. English c. 1800. Both bottom drawers
are false.
W. Stockbridge and Sons Ltd, Cambridge

61 Late eighteenth-century multi-purpose gentleman's wash stand with green baize covered writing drawer. Eighteenth-century chintz curtains and drapes over the immense French domed 'Polonaise' bed.
Biddick Hall, County Durham

These pots come from two magnificent collections: 300 hang from the ceiling of the Oak Tree Inn at Hutton Magna in North Yorkshire, and Joe Painter of Dersingham in Norfolk has over 800 in his garden shed.

62 Royal Doulton turquoise bow and pink rosebud,
c. 1920.
Oak Tree Inn, Hutton Magna, Yorkshire

63 Gold Key Pattern and pink roses,
c. 1900. Possibly Minton.
Oak Tree Inn, Hutton Magna, Yorkshire

64 Turn of the century brown and white
Staffordshire with lid.
Oak Tree Inn, Hutton Magna, Yorkshire

65 Blue daffodil. A pot of 1890 of particularly fine
quality.
Oak Tree Inn, Hutton Magna, Yorkshire

66 Late nineteenth-century green, pink and blue
fuschia design.
Joe Painter, Dersingham, Norfolk

67 The pot cupboard in the drawing room at Flintham Hall in Nottinghamshire. These discreet cupboards in what was formerly the billiard room would be an essential convenience for the gentlemen. The cast is of the Strangford Apollo. The pagodas are eighteenth-century, from the Chinese room at nearby Cliston Hall. The Beehive is a French work box, and a nineteenth-century ostrich egg is held aloft in the middle of the table. The bamboo chamber pot is nineteenth-century.

68 Three nineteenth-century bow
designs. The brown ribbon is the earliest, dating
from 1830. The blue bow, from Sandringham, is
mysteriously called 'Oriental Ivory', with a stamp
of a chinaman under an umbrella. It was potted in
January 1881 by Bishop and Stoner of Hanley. The
red was potted in September 1878 by Brownfield at
Corbridge.
Joe Painter, Dersingham, Norfolk

69 A twentieth-century pot with nasturtium
design.
Joe Painter, Dersingham, Norfolk

70 George V and Queen Mary Coronation
Commemorative Pot of 1911.
Joe Painter, Dersingham, Norfolk

71 1887 Jubilee pot.
Joe Painter, Dersingham, Norfolk

75 One of two commodes belonging to an 1840s Gothic Revival set of bedroom furniture at Raby Castle in County Durham. Made for the Duke of Cleveland with his monogram DC and the Ducal coronet, the set consists of two wash stands, a bedside cabinet, a cheval mirror and these two commodes. The bed too is Gothic Revival of the 1840s with the Coats of Arms of the second Earl of Darlington and his wife Margaret (another on the footboard). The cover is a Marseilles quilt with the Arms of the Prince of Wales, later George IV. The portrait on the left is a Van Dyck of a judge, on the right of the seventeenth-century first Duke of Grafton as a young man. The candle snuffers, inkstand and candle stick are Derby. The mother of pearl blotter is Victorian.

76, 77 and 78 Oddities of twentieth-century chamber pot design. The left-hand hunting scene has 'Palissy, England' stamped on it. No. 78 was decorated by Clarice Cliffe, c. 1930.

79 An example of Belgian Art Nouveau:
'Manufacture Imperiale et Royale Fabrication
Belge'.

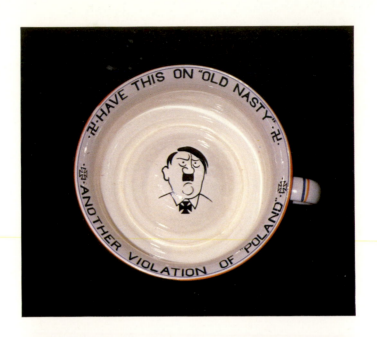

80 and 81 When lifted, 'Rule Britannia'
triumphantly plays.